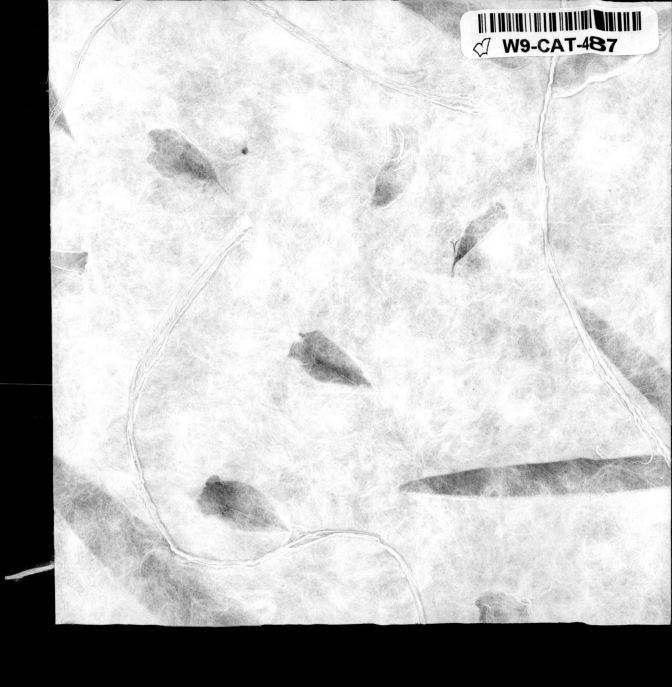

6/09

Dearest Michael,

There are many good things in this life,
but one of the best is knowing that the
rest of my days will be blessed with a
nearness to you.

Susan Channel

One of the best parts of
my life is having you
as my brother.
Love & Blessings.
Susan

Other books in the *"Language of"* Series... by

Blue Mountain Press ®

The Language of Love

The Language of Friendship

The Language of Happiness

The Language of Marriage

The Language of Teaching

The Language of Courage and Inner Strength

Thoughts to Share with a Wonderful Mother

Thoughts to Share with a Wonderful Father

Thoughts to Share with a Wonderful Son

Thoughts to Share with a Wonderful Daughter

It's Great to Have a Sister like You

The "Language of" Series...

It's Great to Have a

BROTHER

like You

A Collection from Blue Mountain Arts®

Edited by Douglas Pagels

Blue Mountain Press ®

Boulder, Colorado

Library of Congress Catalog Card Number: 98-50185
ISBN: 0-88396-492-9

ACKNOWLEDGMENTS appear on page 48.

Manufactured in Thailand
Third Printing: August 1999

 This book is printed on recycled paper.

Library of Congress Cataloging-in-Publication Data

It's great to have a brother like you : a collection from Blue Mountain Arts / edited by Douglas Pagels.

   p. cm. -- ("Language of..." series)
  ISBN 0-88396-492-9 (alk. paper)
  1. Brothers--Literary collections. I. Pagels, Douglas. II. Blue Mountain Arts
(Firm) III. Series.
  PN6071.B78 188 1999
  808.81'9352045--dc21

                                                 98-50185
                                                  CIP
                                                 Rev.

Blue Mountain Press INC.

P.O. Box 4549, Boulder, Colorado 80306

Contents
(Authors listed in order of first appearance)

I would love for you to know
            something, Brother.

I think you're a pretty wonderful guy.
And I know I don't tell you
often enough how much you mean to me,
and how much you always have...
            but you're someone I dearly love.

I think of you a lot, and one thought
that has crossed my mind so many times
is that... of the millions
            of brothers in the world...

I somehow managed to be blessed
    with the best one of all.

 Laurel Atherton

Thanks, Brother

Because you care, each task will be much lighter,
   Each burden so much easier to bear;
And each new morning's outlook better, brighter,
   And each new day more blest, because you care.

Because you care, each joy will seem completer,
   Each treasure doubly dear and true and rare;
And in my heart I'll always find it sweeter...
         Because you care.

 — Dr. Frank Crane

Knowing that you are always
here to understand and accept
me helps me get along in the
confused world. If every person
could have someone just like
you, the world would become
a peaceful garden.

 — Susan Polis Schutz

To My Wonderful Brother

There have been many times in our lives
when we have seemed to be in different worlds.
We are very different in many ways,
but we are also much the same in others,
which is to be expected.
But the most important fact remains:
you can call me at a moment's notice,
and I will drop everything to come to you.

I love you more than I could ever tell you,
and I consider myself very lucky
   that you were born to be my brother.
You are a wonderful gift given to me by God,
and like so many other gifts we receive,
I sometimes forget to be thankful for you.
I'd like you to know that I could never have chosen
a more wonderful brother,
   and I love you more than
you'll ever know.

 — Debbie Avery Pirus

My Brother

My brother is hopelessly generous and confiding. He is myself. Understand me when I say that... I know his purity, honor — what he has been from childhood.

Never have I known a nature of such strength, and such almost childlike innocence. He is of a nature so sweet and perfect that, though I have seen him indignant at moments, I never saw him fretful or irritable — a man who continuously, in every little act of life, is thinking of others...

By all the beatitudes, my brother is blessed. His calmness, serenity, and cheerfulness through all this time has uplifted us all. Where he is, there is no anxiety, no sorrow. My brother's power to console is something peculiar and wonderful...

You cannot conceive how he is beloved.

— Harriet Beecher Stowe

You don't choose your family. They are God's gift to you, as you are to them.

— Desmond Tutu

He who loves his brother abides in the light.

I John 2:10 (NKJV)

To you, so near of kin... In the pathway of my life... you have been my courage and my strength, in all sorts of weather, rain or shine.

 Augustus Field Beard

He who serves
    his brother best
Gets nearer God
    than all the rest.

 Alexander Pope

To the Best Brother in the World

You are one truly special person, special far beyond my ability to express in words. You are one of the most positive people I've ever known. You are such a good person, tough and resilient, but soft and compassionate, and not too proud to change when you think you should. You're a good friend, loyal and loving. You inspire me greatly in all the important decisions of my life. You have a heart of gold. I've never known anyone with such a tender, indomitable spirit.

You helped me shape my ideas when I was growing up. You played a part in my destiny. You taught me to reach for the sky when I might have been satisfied with the ground. You helped me to develop confidence in myself and made me feel I could do anything. You have been a real-life example to me of how never to give up in the face of disappointment, fear, conflict, and trouble.

My life would have been very different without your example, and my days wouldn't be as joyful without your love.

— Donna Fargo

A Brother and His Family

If the family were a container, it would be a nest, an enduring nest, loosely woven, expansive and open.

If the family were a fruit, it would be an orange, a circle of sections, held together but separable — each segment distinct.

If the family were a boat, it would be a canoe that makes no progress unless everyone paddles.

If the family were a sport, it would be baseball; a long, slow, nonviolent game that is never over until the last out.

If the family were a building, it would be an old but solid structure that contains human history, and appeals to those who see... the possibilities.

— Letty Cottin Pogrebin

So much of what is great
has sprung from the closeness
of family ties.

Sir James M. Barrie

All your strength is in your union...
As brothers, live together.

Henry Wadsworth Longfellow

Loving relationships are a
family's best protection against
the challenges of the world.

 Bernie Wiebe

The Strength That Comes from Support Within a Brother's Family

The family... was always like the sea, the milieu that could explain and restore him. When thinking about someone's problems, I almost automatically referred to the family around him. It remains everyone's best hope for safe passage.

— Harvey White, M.D.

Good family life is never an accident
but always an achievement
by those who share it.

— James H. S. Bossard

Having a big brother...
can be like having
a hero in the house.
Someone to look up to.
A doer of daring deeds.
A bold brave
who'll scout the territory ahead
and tell you when to stay behind
and when it's safe to go.

 Adele Faber and Elaine Mazlish

A brother is born to help in time of need.

 Proverbs 17:17 (NLT)

A Brother like That

A college friend of mine named Paul received a new automobile from his brother as a Christmas present. When Paul came out of his office, a young man was walking around the shiny new car, admiring it. "Is this your car, mister?" he asked.

Paul nodded, "My brother gave it to me for Christmas."

The young man looked astounded. "You mean your brother gave it to you, and it didn't cost you anything? Boy, I wish...."

He hesitated, and Paul knew what he was going to wish. He was going to wish he had a brother like that. But what the fellow said jarred Paul all the way down to his heels.

"I wish," the fellow went on, "that I could *be* a brother like that."

C. Roy Angell

Excerpts from the letters of Vincent van Gogh
to his beloved brother, Theo

May our mutual love increase with the years.
I am so glad that we have so many things in
common, not only memories of childhood, but
also that... you know so many people and
places which I know also, and that you have
so much love for nature and art.

I shall certainly try to take care that you shall
never regret your generosity.... Doubly and twice
doubly I appreciate your helping me so faithfully
and strongly.

I think of you so often.... How I wish we might be
together. Before the year is gone, I feel I have to
thank you for all your help and friendship.

Vincent

We're So Much Alike

In form and feature, face and limb,
I grew so like my brother
That folks got taking me for him,
And each for one another.

— Henry Sambrooke Leigh

Family faces are magic mirrors. Looking
at people who belong to us, we see the
past, present, and future.

— Gail Lumet Buckley

These two were so much like one another
that each to each
was more than brother.

 — Ethyl Lynn-Beers

We're So Different

A sibling is both your mirror —
and your opposite.

— Elizabeth Fishel

The differences between us are dramatic, and
yet we are so closely related. Our interests veer
in different directions, and yet our wandering
paths began on the stairs of the same front
porch. And though some say they find a trace
of our faces in one another, it is not clearly so.

But there is one thing I do know, deep inside me:
You are my brother. Much admired, dearly loved.
And someone whose qualities I wish I had more of.

 — Dale Sanborne

Family Ties

It is good to think of you living around me, not
far away, connected with me through darkness
and space by a certain mysterious human cord.

 — Ray Stannard Baker

A Brother's Part in the Family

Successful family living strikes me as being in many ways
rather like playing chamber music. Each member of the
ensemble has his own skills, his own special knack with
the part he chooses to play; but the grace and strength
and sweetness of the performance come from everyone's
willingness to subordinate individual virtuosity and personal
ambition to the requirements of balance and blend.

 — Annis Duff

A happy family is but
an earlier heaven.

 — Sir John Bowring

At Home in My Heart

Even if the times of our lives
should find us many miles apart,
you will never be alone.
I will always be there with you.
And you shall always be here with me.
Your hopes will be my hopes.
Your history will be my history.
Your memories will parallel those
  of my own.

And, any time we choose to go there,
my love for you and your love for me
will meet on a bridge that will
happily take us
          all the way
                  back home.

I love you, Brother.

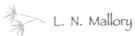 — L. N. Mallory

A Brother Is...

...a friend given by nature.

Jean Baptiste LeGouve

...a peace that comes from knowing,
with loving certainty, that I will always
have someone in this world with whom
I am wonderfully connected. Someone
who is intrinsically — a part of me; and
someone I am a portion of. Someone
to turn to, someone to share with,
someone — always — to love.

Robin Kelsey

...a portion of a beloved bond, born and blessed,
and someone whose influence can be measured
by no human means.

 R. L. Keith

...one of the holiest of gifts. God can bestow
nothing more sacred upon us.

 Tiedge

...understanding and encouragement. Helping out and looking out
for my best interests. There when I need him, no questions asked.
Somebody I didn't appreciate enough in so many days past, but
someone I can't thank enough in the present.

— Ann Turrel

...a being that is willing to bear with us
in all our faults and failings.

George Forster

...more than a brother, more than a friend,
more like a blend — of everything
I'll ever need
someone to be.

 S. J. Ellenson

Brothers can quarrel like thieves inside a house, but outside their swords leap out in each other's defense.

Japanese Proverb

The thing about fighting with your brother...
is you don't stay mad forever.

And even though
you may hit each other
nobody else better try.

And even though
you call each other bad names
nobody else better say anything bad.

Deep inside you know
when trouble comes
and there's no one else to turn to
you can call on each other
and count on each other
to care for each other
because each other
is all you have.

Adele Faber and Elaine Mazlish

We are brothers. Our interests lie along the same lines, helping us to realize that we are not alone. There is no one so capable of protecting a brother... as one who believes what he believes, and reveres the sentiments that are so sacred to him.

Now and then, there may have been occasional differences between us. But in the long run, they have been merely ripples on the ocean. The love which binds us together cannot be severed by anything.

J. S. Caster

A Bond to Last a Lifetime

There are many good things in this life, but one of the best is knowing that the rest of my days will be blessed with a nearness to you.

The ties between siblings are drawn together more closely than we know. Far too often, we don't realize the depth and breadth of that love until the love is called forth in times of need. For then, there is an outpouring. A time when nothing is too much to ask. It is a time of realizing how close, how caring, and how eternal that bond will be.

But just think... how wonderful it would be to realize and recognize that ever-present love during the good times and carefree days. Why wait for moments when everything is on the edge? We could go instead to the center of ourselves. We should find the time and show the way to a place where feelings flow easily into the heart, and where some of the most precious thoughts of all... have to do... with brothers and sisters... and endless gratitude.

 — Susan Channel

May the connection between us always
be filled with the fun of family stories and
the happiness of a wonderful union.

 Orison S. Marden

May my brother be blessed with
the four comforts of life: love,
liberty, health, and contentment.

 Anonymous

In many ways the family is the most demanding training ground that life has to offer. We are born into our families. We do not choose them the way we choose our friends — and often siblings... don't share our values or outlook on life. In fact, they may — and often do — radically disagree with us. They may prove difficult to get along with... and yet we share a bond of common experience, and in most families, a kind of love that is unique in its strength and depth.

Rick Fields

A Brother Is a Very Special Friend

True friendship is a brotherhood of thought,
Knowing no selfishness —
       between heart and heart,
Counting each friendly sacrifice as naught,
Finding context in having done its part...
A beacon smiling over seas of strife,
Blazing a pathway to a tranquil lea;
A glad oasis on the sands of life
Between the cradle and eternity.

 Elton D. Spink

The Entire World Changes When a Brother Comes into Your Life

After a male baby has grown out of diapers and has acquired pants, freckles, and so much dirt that relatives dare not kiss it between meals, it becomes a "brother." A brother is Nature's answer to that false belief that there is no such thing as perpetual motion. A brother can swim like a fish, run like a deer, climb like a squirrel, bellow like a bull, and eat like a pig, according to climatic conditions.

He is a piece of skin stretched over an appetite. A noise covered with smudges. He is a tornado because he comes in at the most unexpected times, hits the most unexpected places, and leaves everything behind him. He is a growing boy of superlative promise, to be fed, watered, and kept warm...

Were it not for brothers, the funny papers would go unread and a thousand picture shows would go bankrupt. Brothers are useful in running errands... but his zest in doing so is often equaled only by the speed of a turtle on a July day.

A brother is a natural spectator. He watches parades, fires, ball games, automobiles, boats, and airplanes with equal fervor, but he will not watch the clock. A brother, if not washed too often and if kept in a cool, quiet place after each accident, will survive broken bones, hornets, swimming pools, and numerous helpings of pie.

A brother is evidence that God is not yet discouraged of man.
A brother is a joy forever.

Anonymous

The spiritual interpretation of life teaches
us that all human life is sacred;
that we are members one of another;
that the things which we have in common
are greater than those which divide;
that each is his brother's keeper.

 W. L. MacKenzie King

Brothers are sometimes dependent upon
each other for happiness.... When a brother
falls and the question is asked, "Am I my
brother's keeper?" — it is answered that
there is a sacred trust to perform... for
the welfare of a brother.

D. C. Smith

The answer to the question, "Am I my
brother's keeper?" must always be,
"No, I am my brother's brother."

 Paul Klapper

Of Brotherhood

Grant us brotherhood, not only for this day but for all our years — a brotherhood not of words but of acts and deeds.

 — Stephen Vincent Benet

Help thy brother's boat across, and lo! Thine own has reached the shore.

— Hindu Proverb

Be human, and loving, and gentle, and brotherly all the while.

 — William Morley Punshon

To My Brother

We have... the relationship of family and the strong band of personal friendship. So many times we have acted together, and with our united effort, we have achieved what at first seemed impossible.

J. S. Caster

How wonderful it is, how pleasant, when brothers live together in harmony.

Psalms 133:1 (NLT)

You watched these people go through their lives and just had a feeling that they existed outside the usual laws of nature.... There was endless action — not just football, but sailboats, tennis, and other things: movement. There was endless talk... but everyone weighing in with their opinions and taking part. It was as simple as this... they were a unit.

— Charles Spalding, writing about
the Kennedy brothers

The ties of the family teach us to love one another... with simplicity, confidence, and kindness.

 Anonymous

Grasp the hand of brotherly love.

 J. B. Sullivan

Dearest brother, I thank you a thousand times.
I still do not know to this day what to say
about my plans... and now the only question is
whether I shall see you again soon. Say "Yes"
to this; I believe you would do me more good
than all my medicine.
My love to you... and continue
your love for me.

 Felix Mendelssohn

I recognize in you a true brother.
I pay to you my tribute of love and
affection, and I clasp your hand
with devotion and pride.

J. B. Sullivan

You Are a Wonderful Brother

You (one of the people who knows me best)
need to know how proud I am to have you
as my brother.

You (who understands me so well) need to
understand how much the presence of your
life has added to my happiness.

You (who inspires me so much) need to
realize what an inspiration you are to the
bright and shining hopes I keep in my heart.

And you (who is such an important part of
my past) need to remember that I'm going
to be grateful for you...
with a love and a thanks
that will last forever.

 Gillian Reese

What Makes Us Siblings?

Nurtured in the same dark womb
sired by one father
held close by one mother
reared under the same roof
steeped in the same traditions
sung the same songs,
we share a double line of ancestors
that reached back to the beginning of time.
Each, part of the past
part of father
part of mother
part of each other.
Echoes of each other's being.
Whose eyes are those that look like mine?
Whose smile reminds me of my own?
Whose thoughts come through
    with just a glance?
Who knows me as no others do?
Who in the whole wide world
    is most like me
yet not like me at all?
My sibling.

— Adele Faber and Elaine Mazlish

Impressive and lovely is the idea of being
linked together with a brother in kindred
companionship. Love, friendship and
helpfulness are the offspring of a happier
environment where brothers and sisters...
help each other to live happy and useful lives.

 J. W. Mackay

Thank heaven for those who have always
known us.... We belong to each other
and always shall.

 Sarah Orne Jewett

My Brother, My Friend

In his play *As You Like It*, Shakespeare tells us that, "One man in his time plays many parts." Surely this will be true of you in your life. Your many talents and abilities will take you down various paths and lead you to many different types of challenges and destinations. It is my prayer for you that they all lead to joy, health, and success.

When you are older, and you look back at all the parts you have played in your lifetime, you may see that you have indeed played many roles, those of: son, student, teenager, young man, graduate, employee, husband, father, uncle, and even grandfather...

When you look in the mirror, you see only yourself — as you know yourself to be. But there is much more going on in that mirror. It's a reflection that has no limitations and that has many definitions and meanings. You look... and see you. But others see you through their own eyes, their own background, their circumstances and unique perspectives.

What you are and what you will always be is an amazing composite of many things. In the course of your life, you will have many hats to wear, many family dynamics to experience, and many roles to play. You will have a multifaceted life filled with faces, names, and places that will be an integral part of everything that you are. But within all those roles that you will play, there are two that — for me — will be the most wonderful among them.

And that is having you as my brother
...and having you as my friend.

Douglas Pagels

Blessed is he who loves his brother
as well when he is afar off as when
he is by his side.

St. Francis of Assisi

Where'er I roam, whatever
realms to see,
My heart untravell'd
fondly turns to thee...
my brother.

Oliver Goldsmith

Brother, You Are the Best

There are years lost behind us, full of words we never spoke, and now we have our separate lives and less time to share together. But in my heart I have always felt the love we have, and neither distance nor time can take away the bond we forged as children.

Growing up, we played and fought, talked and laughed. Beyond the fun and games, beyond the battles we waged, we found in each other unending support and a lifelong friend. Through thick and thin, and difficult times, we emerged together as one, protecting each other from the world. I know that if either of us ever needs anything, we can count on the other to give their all and help in every way possible.

Perhaps words are not always necessary in our relationship, because we both know what's there. But today I want to take the time to remind you how much I really care and thank you for all that you have been to me. I could never ask for, want, or need a better brother, because I have the best in you.

I love you!

 — Erin N. Himelrick

There is a destiny that makes us brothers;
   None goes his way alone:
All that we send into the lives of others
   Comes back into our own.

               Edwin Markham

To a Brother,
with Love Through It All

In all our losses, all our gains,
In all our pleasures, all our pains,
The life of life is: Love remains.

          Wilfrid Gibson

We know that friendship may change...
and even love may be transformed,
but the cords one has with a brother
are never severed.

          Edwin Burdick

To My Wonderful Brother

I feel so secure
knowing that you
are always ready
if I need you
to protect me
to help me
or just to talk to me
I hope you know that
I am always here for you also

It is such a
nice feeling
to have a brother like you
with whom I have grown up
and who will always stay
   in my life
with strength
with understanding
and with love
I love you

Susan Polis Schutz

ACKNOWLEDGMENTS

We gratefully acknowledge the permission granted by the following authors, publishers, and authors' representatives to reprint poems or excerpts from their publications.

Lynn C. Franklin Associates, Ltd. for "You don't choose..." by Desmond Tutu from SIMPSON'S CONTEMPORARY QUOTATIONS compiled by James B. Simpson, published by Houghton Mifflin Company, Inc. Copyright © by Lynn C. Franklin Associates, Ltd. All rights reserved. Reprinted by permission.

PrimaDonna Entertainment Corp. for "To the Best Brother in the World" by Donna Fargo. Copyright © 1999 by PrimaDonna Entertainment Corp. All rights reserved. Reprinted by permission.

G. P. Putnam's Sons, a division of Penguin Putnam, Inc., for from "The Thing About Fighting" and "What Makes Us Siblings?" from BETWEEN BROTHERS AND SISTERS by Adele Faber and Elaine Mazlish. Copyright © 1989 by Adele Faber, Elaine Mazlish, and The Philip Lief Group, Inc. All rights reserved. Reprinted by permission.

The Sunday School Board for "A Brother like That" from BASKETS OF SILVER by C. Roy Angell. Copyright © 1955 by Broadman Press, Nashville, TN. All rights reserved. Reprinted by permission of The Sunday School Board.

Alfred A. Knopf, Inc. for "Family faces..." by Gail Lumet Buckley from SIMPSON'S CONTEMPORARY QUOTATIONS compiled by James B. Simpson, published by Houghton Mifflin Company, Inc. Copyright © by Alfred A. Knopf, Inc. All rights reserved. Reprinted by permission of Alfred A. Knopf, Inc.

Gramercy Books, Inc. for "Grant us brotherhood..." by Stephen Vincent Benet from WORDS OF WISDOM by Philanthropic Service for Institutions. Copyright © 1993 by Philanthropic Service for Institutions. All rights reserved. Reprinted by permission of Gramercy Books, Inc.

Scripture quotations marked (NLT) are taken from the Holy Bible, New Living Translation, copyright © 1996. Used by permission of Tyndale House Publishers, Inc., Wheaton, Illinois 60189. All rights reserved.

A careful effort has been made to trace the ownership of poems and excerpts used in this anthology in order to obtain permission to reprint copyrighted materials and give proper credit to the copyright owners. If any error or omission has occurred, it is completely inadvertent, and we would like to make corrections in future editions provided that written notification is made to the publisher:

BLUE MOUNTAIN PRESS, INC., P.O. Box 4549, Boulder, Colorado 80306.